ALLIGATORS AND CROCODILES

BY ELLIS M. REED

The Child's World®
childsworld.com

Published by The Child's World®
1980 Lookout Drive • Mankato, MN 56003-1705
800-599-READ • www.childsworld.com

Photographs ©: iStockphoto, cover (alligator), 2, 8, 9, 20, 24 (alligator); Shutterstock Images, cover (crocodile), 2, 15, 21, 24 (crocodile); Ning Je taime/ Shutterstock Images, 5; Joseph M. Arseneau/ Shutterstock Images, 6; Orhan Cam/Shutterstock Images, 10; Alizada Studios/Shutterstock Images, 13; Sergey Uryadnikov/Shutterstock Images, 14; Nataliia Melnychuk/Shutterstock Images, 17; Kajornyot Wildlife Photography, 19

ISBN 9781503835900
LCCN 2019942972

Printed in the United States of America

ABOUT THE AUTHOR

Ellis M. Reed writes and edits children's books. When she lived in Florida, an alligator lived in her backyard.

TABLE OF CONTENTS

CHAPTER

1

Sharp Teeth

A **reptile** swims in the water. It has a long tail. It has sharp claws and teeth. It raises its long **snout** out of the water. Is it an alligator or a crocodile? How are they different?

Crocodiles are powerful hunters.

Most of an alligator's teeth cannot be seen when its mouth is closed.

CHAPTER

2

Alligators

Alligators live in freshwater rivers and lakes. Alligators only live in parts of the United States and China. They can be dark green, brown, or gray. They have round snouts that look like a **U**. They have many teeth. Their side teeth cannot be seen when an alligator closes its mouth.

Alligators are **carnivores**. They eat meat. They eat fish, birds, other reptiles, and small **mammals**.

The Chinese alligator can only be found in the wild near the Yangtze river in China.

Baby alligators stay with their
mother for at least a year.

Baby alligators hatch from eggs. The nest is on land. It is made out of leaves and dirt. This keeps the eggs dry and safe.

The mother alligator carries her **hatchlings** to the water. She carries them in her mouth. Baby alligators stay with their mother for one to three years. She keeps them safe while they grow up.

CHAPTER

3

Crocodiles

Crocodiles live in salt water or **brackish** water such as oceans and **deltas**. Crocodiles live in warm places all over the world. They can be light green or gray. They have narrow snouts that look like a **V**. A crocodile's many teeth can be seen when it closes its mouth.

A crocodile's teeth show even with its mouth closed.

Saltwater crocodiles will hunt anything that comes near them.

Crocodiles are also carnivores. They eat many kinds of **prey**, including fish and small mammals.

Baby crocodiles also hatch from eggs. The nest is in a mound or hole under the sand. This keeps the eggs dry and safe.

The mother crocodile helps her babies to the water. But she does not stay long. She leaves after a few days. Then the baby crocodiles are on their own.

Baby crocodiles have to take care of themselves.

CHAPTER

4

What's the Difference?

Alligators live in fresh water. Crocodiles live in salt water or brackish water. Alligator teeth are hidden when they close their mouths. Crocodile teeth can still be seen. Alligators stay with their babies for a few years. Crocodiles only stay with their babies for a few days.

Both alligators and crocodiles eat meat. They both live in the water. They have a lot in common. And they are both fearsome reptiles.

ALLIGATORS

- Live in fresh water
- Mothers stay with babies for one to three years
- Only found in the United States and China

CROCODILES

- Live in salt water or brackish water
- Mothers leave babies after a few days
- Found in warm places all over the world

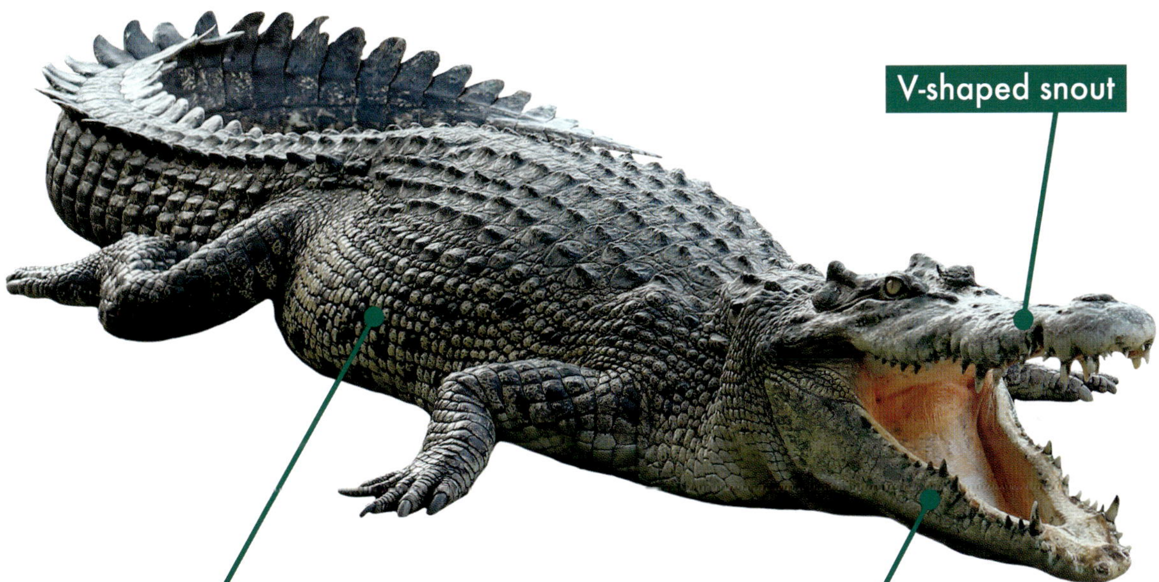

GLOSSARY

brackish (BRAK-ish) Brackish water is a mix of salt water and fresh water. Some crocodiles live in brackish water.

carnivores (KAR-nih-vorz) Carnivores are animals that eat meat. Alligators are carnivores.

deltas (DEL-tuhz) Deltas are where fast moving water, such as rivers, meets slow moving water, such as oceans. Crocodiles sometimes make their homes in deltas.

hatchlings (HACH-lings) Hatchlings are animals that have just hatched from eggs. A mother alligator carries her hatchlings in her mouth.

mammals (MAM-ulz) Mammals are animals that have hair and give birth to live young. Crocodiles and alligators eat small mammals.

prey (PRAY) Prey are animals that are eaten by other animals. Alligators eat prey such as other reptiles and fish.

reptile (REP-tyl) A reptile is a scaly animal that is cold-blooded, meaning it cannot control its body temperature and has to use the sun to keep warm. A crocodile is a reptile.

snout (SNOWT) A snout is an animal's nose. Alligators have round snouts.

TO LEARN MORE

IN THE LIBRARY

Herrington, Lisa M. *Crocodiles and Alligators*. New York, NY: Scholastic, 2016.

Marsh, Laura. *Alligators and Crocodiles*. Washington, DC: National Geographic Society, 2015.

Spalding, Maddie. *The Animal Life Cycle*. Mankato, MN: The Child's World, 2019.

ON THE WEB

Visit our website for links about alligators and crocodiles:
childsworld.com/links

Note to Parents, Teachers, and Librarians: We routinely verify our Web links to make sure they are safe and active sites. So encourage your readers to check them out!

ACTIVITY

Draw a picture of an alligator and a crocodile. Your picture should clearly show the differences between the alligator and the crocodile. Look at pages 20 and 21 for help.

INDEX